PRAISE FOR

Child Consecration: To Jesus through Mary—Following in the Spirit of St. Thérèse, the Little Flower

Child Consecration: To Jesus through Mary—Following in the Spirit of St. Thérèse the Little Flower is a wonderful means by which children can come to know God's Blessed Mother in an easy and accessible way. By re-proposing St. Louis de Montfort's classic work *True Devotion to Mary*, young minds and hearts will be opened to receive the tender love of Mary and be brought to an encounter with her Son, Jesus Christ. I commend this book to parents and teachers, who will find here a solid and ready means to develop the spiritual and devotional life of children, giving them a firm foundation from which to build their relationship with the Lord and his Church.

—HIS EMINENCE ROBERT CARDINAL SARAH
Prefect of the Congregation for Divine Worship
and the Discipline of the Sacraments

Saint Louis de Montfort in his *True Devotion to the Blessed Virgin Mary* provides the solid foundation of Catholic devotion to the Virgin Mother of God whom her Divine Son has given to us as our Mother in the Church. Countless Catholics have followed the way of consecration, proposed by Saint Louis, to their great and lasting spiritual benefit. *Child Consecration to Jesus through Mary*, while remaining faithful to the teaching of Saint Louis de Montfort, makes it accessible for children. I highly recommend it to parents who wish to introduce their children to Marian devotion and thus help them to give their hearts, one with the Immaculate Heart of Mary, completely to the Sacred Heart of Jesus.

—HIS EMINENCE RAYMOND LEO CARDINAL BURKE

I congratulate Blythe Kaufman for this commendable and outstanding book, *Child Consecration: To Jesus Through Mary—Following in the Spirit of St. Thérèse, the Little Flower*. The main thrust of this consecration book is to equip children and adults of our times in their journey of life. The topics for the thirty-three days are logically connected and appropriate for every day's meditation in a simple way, not only for children but also for adults. I personally believe that following or using this consecration book will encourage individuals and families to deepen their spiritual life. I therefore seize this opportunity to recommend highly *Child Consecration: To Jesus through Mary* for priests, religious, seminaries, children, youth, adults, Catholic parishes and Catholic schools.

—MOST REV. PHILIP DAVOU DUNG,
Bishop of Shendam, Nigeria

It is my fervent wish that through this book, *Child Consecration: To Jesus through Mary—Following in the Spirit of St. Thérèse, the Little Flower*, young Catholics will be drawn more to a life of holiness through the intercession of the Blessed Virgin Mary and become agents of transformation in society.

—MOST REV. REYNALDO G. EVANGELISTA, DD,
Bishop of Imus, Philippines

As human beings, we are all called to live a life of holiness—a life easily attained and lived through the motherly guidance of the Blessed Virgin Mary. This is a life which is fruitfully nurtured at our early stage of life as children. This book presents to children the true devotion to the Blessed Virgin Mary which leads to a deeper and more perfect devotion to Jesus who calls all to a life of holiness. I commend this book to all who nurture the tender souls of children—the future of the Church, for through it they will be able to introduce many to the Mother of God who opens great realities of the faith to the simple hearted, especially children, and also searches for them when lost.

—MOST REV. PAUL SSEMOGERERE,
Bishop of Kasana-Luweero, Uganda

In her new book *Child Consecration: To Jesus through Mary—Following in the Spirit of St. Thérèse, the Little Flower*, the tireless Children's Rosary champion, Blythe Kaufman, focuses her devotional spirit on the time-honored practice of Consecrating our children to Jesus through Mary. Beautifully illustrated, the book delights as it instructs, drawing us closer to Our Lady and ultimately her Son.

—DOUG KECK, EWTN President and Chief Operating Officer,
Host of EWTN Bookmark

Child Consecration

To Jesus through Mary—

Following in the Spirit of St. Thérèse, the Little Flower

by
Blythe Kaufman, DMD, MDS

Illustrated by Abigail Ryan

© Copyright 2020
Blythe Kaufman, DMD, MDS
All Rights Reserved
Printed in the United States of America

Published with Ecclesiastical approval
Permission to publish granted by the Most Rev. Leonard P. Blair, Archbishop of Hartford, July 28, 2020.

All Bible references were taken from the New American Bible Revised Edition (New Jersey: Catholic Book Publishing Corp., 1986).

All *Catechism* quotations were taken from the *Catechism of the Catholic Church* (New York: Doubleday, 1994).

No part of this book may be reproduced or transmitted, in any form or by any means, without permission.

The cover illustration was painted by Abigail Ryan at age nine. She is a member of the Children's Rosary prayer group movement. She painted it initially to serve as a Christmas card for the Children's Rosary. Yet it seemed the Lord and Our Lady had more plans for this image. From the beginning there was an appreciation for the face of Our Blessed Mother in the painting. There was something incredibly gentle in the face of Our Lady. It was full of love and tenderness. In the simplicity of a child's hand, Our Lady was brought to life as the most loving of mothers presenting her Son, Jesus. The cover of this book serves as a witness to the beauty of the hearts of children and how much they can do.

For more information please visit
www.childconsecration.com

This book is dedicated to the Holy Trinity and Our Blessed Mother. This book is also dedicated to St. John Paul II, St. Thérèse, St. Louis de Montfort, St. Joseph, St. Michael, and the Holy Angels in gratitude for their intercession.

True Devotion to Mary

It is tender; that is, full of confidence in her, like a child's confidence in his loving mother. [1]

-St. Louis de Montfort

True devotion to Mary leads to a deeper and more perfect devotion to Jesus. It is the moor line of our boats at sea that leads us to the safe harbor of our true home in Heaven.

Foreword

From my earliest years my mother used to remind me, albeit on occasion, how she consecrated me and my siblings in the first days after our birth to Our Lady, at Her Altar in our local parish church. I do not imagine this act on mum's part was an altogether common practice at the time but, then again, it was certainly far from unheard of in the mid-1960s when I entered the world. In fact the custom was a settled feature in the treasury of the Church's devotional life. From time to time, whenever I have had cause to call to mind this childhood Marian consecration I have felt some supernatural comfort and assurance. More than that, I have even pondered whether the contours of my vocation as a priest, and now bishop, were not marked out there and then in that simple act of entrustment to Our Lady of an ordinary Catholic mother. How many souls I wonder were saved, and saints crafted, by other countless maternal acts of consecration of the young to the Mother of Jesus, and Mother of mothers.

Taking up Blythe Kaufman's *Child Consecration: To Jesus through Mary* reminded me fondly of my own childhood consecration. It was like going through an old desk and coming across some *memento* of a by-gone age that, to my surprise, had lost none of its freshness or poignancy, relevance and vitality. *Child Consecration* reminds me of Jesus' words about the: *scribe discipled in the Kingdom of Heaven who brings out of his storeroom treasures old and new.*

I encourage every parent, teacher and priest to read this book, quite unique in these times, that accompanies parents as they take up again the devotion of consecrating their children to Jesus through Mary. This thirty-three day consecration, designed for elementary school children, follows Saint Louis-Marie de Montfort's Consecration to Jesus through Mary but in a way appropriated to children, following the spirit of simplicity, confidence and trust of Saint Thérèse of Lisieux. Beneath the author's simple style there lies a profound spiritual soul, full of the practical wisdom of an attentive mother of faith.

Everything is founded on the story of a child guided by her mother to tend her father's garden, a story that engages the imagination and senses, and that is complimented by quite exquisite illustrations that lift the spirits with their innocent joy. That said, this story represents a comprehensive Christian allegory that goes on to unfold, day by day through the consecration journey: the panorama of the Scriptures; the wisdom of the Church; its elementary catechesis; its treasury of Holy Mass and the Sacraments; its essential prayers and devotions; its training in virtue, and all in the service of forming characters and personalities in light of the Christian vision of the human person. The realism with which Original Sin and redeeming grace are taken into account has created a quite exceptional manual for leading today's children safely to Jesus around the pitfalls and temptations that abound in our modern culture.

Child Consecration is a delightful book that seems effortlessly to help parents and children scale to great heights in a consecration to Jesus through Mary as real as that proposed by Saint Louis-Marie de Montfort to the most mature of Christian souls.

Were I a parent, this would be my number one Marian book for my family. As a pastor of souls I pray many parents will take it up, confident that it has within it the grace to bring in a great harvest for the Church and the world in the generations too that lie ahead.

Most Rev. John Keenan
Bishop of Paisley, Scotland

Preface

Bringing the baptized children closer to Christ and creating a fertile climate in which the grace they have received in baptism can bear richer fruit is a sacred task for the Church. The path of deepening faith is not a lonely path, but it leads us deeper into the community of the Church. Mary is standing in the middle of this community.

We go to Jesus by her hand. For many it has already been shown that the devotion to our Blessed Lady is a fertile breeding ground for developing a richer devotion to Jesus Christ. Many saints have pointed out this way, especially by St. Louis Grignon de Montfort (1673-1716), of whom St. John Paul II was a convinced follower.

The author of this book wanted to open for children the possibility of an entrustment to Mary, with a thorough preparation. She was inspired by both St. Louis de Montfort and St. John Paul II. Moreover, in this preparation process she has given much attention to the working of the Holy Spirit, with whom the Blessed Virgin Mary has such a special bond.

May the way of prayer and entrustment presented in this book be a rich blessing for many children.

His Eminence Willem Jacobus Cardinal Eijk
+ Archbishop of Utrecht

Introduction

St. Thérèse wrote in her autobiography, "God gave me the consolation of contemplating at close range the souls of little children." She reflected, "Seeing innocent souls at such close range, I understand what a misfortune it was when they were not formed in their early years, when they are soft as wax upon which one can imprint either virtue or vice." [2]

Indeed, an innocent soul is precious. St. Dominic Savio, who died at the early age of fourteen, was known for his gentle and kind soul. His virtue was well developed, and he was known to help others living at the Oratory with St. John Bosco along the path of virtue. In his memoirs, St. John Bosco reported a vision he had while sleeping of St. Dominic Savio. The boy was leading other children in Heaven. He was clothed in garments with jewels and flowers that gave honor to the purity he maintained within his soul. When St. John Bosco asked St. Dominic what was his greatest consolation at the time of death, Dominic replied, "What helped me most and gave me greatest joy when I was dying was the loving care and help of the great Mother of God. Tell your sons not to fail to keep close to her while they are alive. But hurry—the time is almost up." [3]

Thus, we see there is indeed a window of opportunity to cultivate tender young souls in virtue when such work is gentle and well received. Our Lord sends us help with such an important task. He sends us His Mother to help in cultivating holiness in His children. Our Lady, in her humility, never forces her help upon anyone, but waits to be asked. This Consecration journey to Jesus through

Mary is the request we make to Mary to bring a soul entrusted to her under her mantle of protection. The soul brings all it has—past, present and future—to be placed at the disposal of Mary. In turn Our Lady takes the soul by the hand and guides it to its true home in Heaven while cultivating a multitude of fruits.

The Consecration is one with an ultimate end leading to Jesus. As Jesus is one with the Father, and the Breath between the two is the Holy Spirit, then essentially the Consecration brings a soul to closer union with God in His Three Persons (cf. *Catechism* 703).

Format and Outline for the Consecration Journey

Format

This Consecration journey follows the format proposed by St. Louis de Montfort. The foundation of St. Louis de Montfort's Consecration is the book *True Devotion to Mary*. The Consecration journey included here seeks to unpack this classic book in a way young people can understand. *Child Consecration: To Jesus through Mary—Following in the Spirit of St. Thérèse, the Little Flower* weaves the principal components of the St. Louis de Montfort Consecration through a lens of spirituality identified with St. Thérèse, the Little Flower. It is characterized by simplicity, confidence, and trust.

Outline

The Consecration journey will consist of 33 consecutive days of readings and prayers followed on the 34th day with a Consecration to Jesus through Mary. The Consecration preparation can be started at any time, but we do recommend, as St. Louis de Montfort did, that the 33rd day of preparation end on a vigil of a Marian feast. Suggested feast days for one's Consecration are provided below but one can conclude on any Marian feast.

Start of the 33 Days	Marian Feast	Consecration/Feast Day
January 9	Our Lady of Lourdes	February 11
February 20*	The Annunciation	March 25
April 10	Our Lady of Fatima	May 13
April 28	The Visitation	May 31
May 25	Our Lady of Perpetual Help	June 27
varies	Blessed Virgin Mary, Mother of the Church	Monday after Pentecost
varies	Immaculate Heart	Saturday after Corpus Christi
June 13	Our Lady of Mount Carmel	July 16
July 13	The Assumption	August 15
July 20	Queenship of Mary	August 22
July 24	Our Lady of Czestochowa	August 26
August 6	Nativity of Mary	September 8
August 10	The Most Holy Name of Mary	September 12
August 13	Our Lady of Sorrows	September 15
September 4	Our Lady of the Rosary	October 7
October 19	Presentation of the Blessed Virgin Mary	November 21
November 5	Immaculate Conception	December 8
November 9	Our Lady of Guadalupe	December 12
November 29	Mother of God	January 1
December 6	Our Lady of Prompt Succor	January 8
December 31	Presentation of the Lord	February 2

*Begin February 21 when there is a leap year and February has 29 days.

    The Consecration journey will begin with the central story (allegory) read on day one. Each day will begin with a prayer to the Holy Spirit and contain a reading. At the conclusion of each reading, there is a goal where the essence of the passage is distilled into a sentence. Following the reading of the goal, there are some additional prayers.

Prayers That Will Be Used during the Consecration Journey

Come, Holy Spirit

Come, Holy Spirit, fill the hearts of Thy faithful and enkindle in them the fire of Thy love.

V. Send forth Thy Spirit, and they shall be created;
R. And Thou shalt renew the face of the earth.
LET US PRAY.
O God, who didst teach the hearts of Thy faithful people by sending them the light of Thy Holy Spirit, grant us by the same Spirit to have right judgement in all things, and evermore to rejoice in His holy comfort. Through Christ Our Lord. Amen
O Holy Spirit, sweet Guest of my soul, abide in me and grant that I may ever abide in Thee.

Our Father

Our Father, Who art in Heaven, hallowed be Thy Name. Thy Kingdom come. Thy Will be done, on earth as it is in Heaven. Give us this day our daily bread. And forgive us our trespasses, as we forgive those who trespass against us. And lead us not into temptation, but deliver us from evil. Amen.

Hail Mary

Hail Mary, full of grace, the Lord is with thee; blessed art thou among women, and blessed is the fruit of thy womb, Jesus. Holy Mary, Mother of God, pray for us sinners, now and at the hour of our death. Amen.

Glory Be to the Father

Glory Be to the Father, and to the Son, and to the Holy Spirit. As it was in the beginning, is now, and will be forever. Amen.

Ave Maris Stella

Hail, bright star of the ocean,
God's own Mother blest,
Ever sinless Virgin,
Gate of heavenly rest.

Taking that sweet *Ave*
Which from Gabriel came,
Peace confirm within us,
Changing Eve's name.

Break the captives' fetters,
Make our blindness day,
Chase all evils from us,
For all blessings pray.

Show thyself a Mother,
May the Word Divine
Born for us thine Infant
Hear our prayers through thine.

Virgin all excelling,
Mildest of the mild,
Free from guilt, preserve us,
Meek and undefiled.

Keep our life all spotless,
Make our way secure,
Till we find in Jesus,
Joy for evermore.

Praise to God the Father,
Honor to the Son,
In the Holy Spirit,
Be the glory one. Amen.

Complete Prayers of the Rosary with Diagram

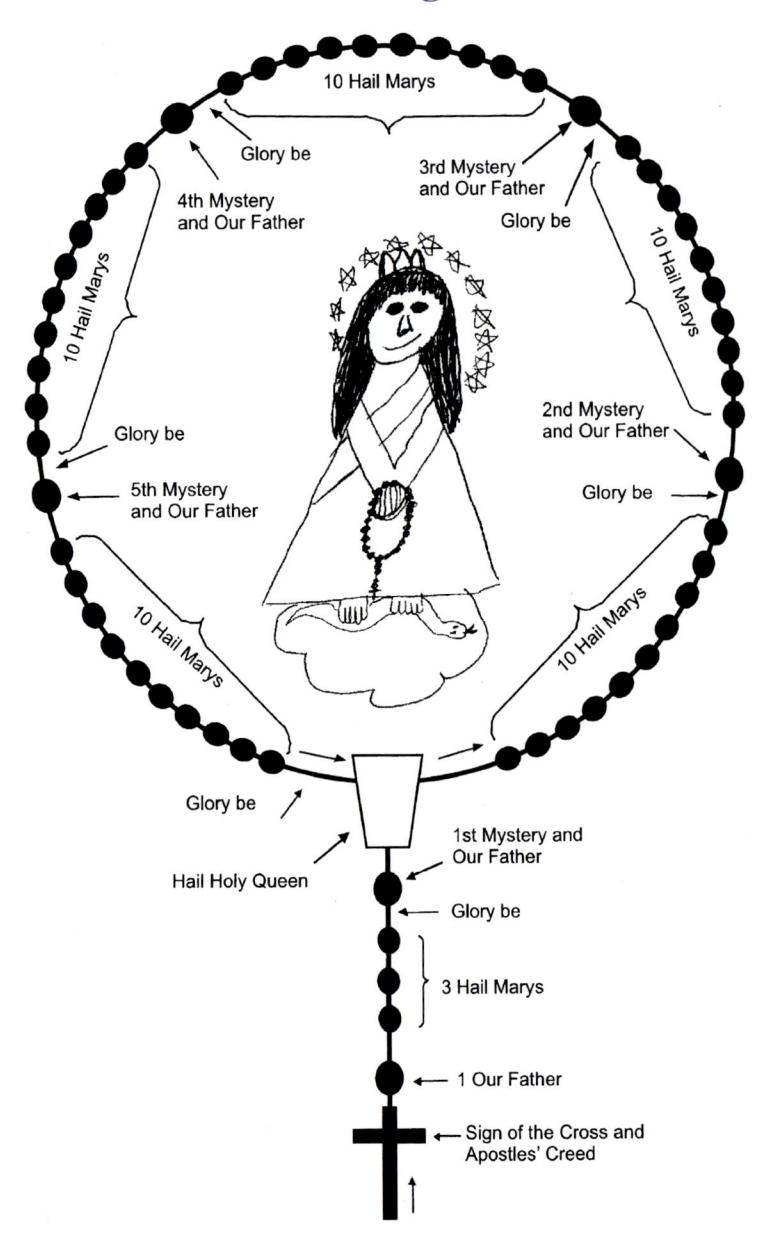

- 10 Hail Marys
- Glory be
- 3rd Mystery and Our Father
- 4th Mystery and Our Father
- Glory be
- 10 Hail Marys
- 10 Hail Marys
- Glory be
- 2nd Mystery and Our Father
- 5th Mystery and Our Father
- Glory be
- 10 Hail Marys
- 10 Hail Marys
- Glory be
- 1st Mystery and Our Father
- Hail Holy Queen
- Glory be
- 3 Hail Marys
- 1 Our Father
- Sign of the Cross and Apostles' Creed

14

Sign of the Cross

In the name of the Father, and of the Son, and of the Holy Spirit. Amen. (As you say this, with your right hand touch your forehead when you say "Father," touch your breastbone when you say "Son," touch your left shoulder when you say "Holy," and touch your right shoulder when you say "Spirit.")

The Apostles' Creed

I believe in God, the Father Almighty, Creator of Heaven and earth; and in Jesus Christ, His only Son Our Lord, Who was conceived by the Holy Spirit, born of the Virgin Mary, suffered under Pontius Pilate, was crucified, died, and was buried. He descended into Hell; the third day He rose again from the dead; He ascended into Heaven, and sitteth at the right hand of God, the Father almighty; from thence He shall come to judge the living and the dead. I believe in the Holy Spirit, the holy Catholic Church, the communion of saints, the forgiveness of sins, the resurrection of the body, and life everlasting. Amen.

Our Father

Our Father, Who art in Heaven, hallowed be Thy Name. Thy kingdom come. Thy Will be done, on earth as it is in Heaven. Give us this day our daily bread. And forgive us our trespasses, as we forgive those who trespass against us. And lead us not into temptation, but deliver us from evil. Amen.

Hail Mary

Hail Mary, full of grace, the Lord is with thee; blessed art thou among women, and blessed is the fruit of thy womb, Jesus. Holy Mary, Mother of God, pray for us sinners, now and at the hour of our death. Amen.

Glory Be to the Father

Glory Be to the Father, and to the Son, and to the Holy Spirit. As it was in the beginning, is now, and will be forever. Amen.

Hail, Holy Queen

Hail, Holy Queen, Mother of mercy; our life, our sweetness, and our hope. To thee do we cry, poor banished children of Eve. To thee do we send up our sighs, mourning and weeping in this vale of tears. Turn, then, most gracious advocate, thine eyes of mercy toward us. And after this, our exile, show unto us the blessed fruit of thy womb, Jesus. O clement, O loving, O sweet Virgin Mary.

Pray for us, O holy Mother of God, that we may be made worthy of the promises of Christ.

Mysteries of the Rosary with the Fruits

On Monday and Saturday, meditate on the *Joyful Mysteries*
First Decade:
The Annunciation of Gabriel to Mary (*Lk* 1:26-38)
FRUIT: HUMILITY
Second Decade: The Visitation of
Mary to Elizabeth (*Lk* 1:39-56)
FRUIT: LOVE OF NEIGHBOR
Third Decade: The Birth of Our Lord (*Lk* 2:1-21)
FRUIT: POVERTY
Fourth Decade: The Presentation of Our Lord (*Lk* 2:22-38)
FRUIT: OBEDIENCE
Fifth Decade: The Finding of
Our Lord in the Temple (*Lk* 2:41-52)
FRUIT: JOY IN FINDING JESUS

On Thursday, meditate on the *Luminous Mysteries*
First Decade: The Baptism of
Our Lord in the River Jordan (*Mt* 3:13-17)
FRUIT: OPENNESS TO THE HOLY SPIRIT
Second Decade: The Wedding at Cana, when
Christ manifested Himself (*Jn* 2:1-11)
FRUIT: TO JESUS THROUGH MARY
Third Decade: The Proclamation of
the Kingdom of God (*Mk* 1:14-15)
FRUIT: REPENTANCE AND TRUST IN GOD
Fourth Decade: The Transfiguration of
Our Lord (*Mt* 17:1-8)
FRUIT: DESIRE FOR HOLINESS
Fifth Decade: The Last Supper, when
Our Lord gave us the Holy Eucharist (*Mt* 26:26-30)
FRUIT: ADORATION

On Tuesday and Friday, meditate on the *Sorrowful Mysteries*
First Decade:
The Agony of Our Lord in the Garden (*Mt 26:36-56*)
FRUIT: SORROW FOR OUR SINS
Second Decade: Our Lord is Scourged at the Pillar (*Mt 27:26*)
FRUIT: PURITY
Third Decade: Our Lord is Crowned with Thorns (*Mt 27:27-31*)
FRUIT: COURAGE
Fourth Decade: Our Lord Carries the Cross to Calvary (*Mt 27:32*)
FRUIT: PATIENCE
Fifth Decade: The Crucifixion of Our Lord (*Mt 27:33-56*)
FRUIT: PERSEVERANCE

On Wednesday and Sunday, meditate on the *Glorious Mysteries*
First Decade: The Glorious Resurrection of Our Lord (*Jn 20:1-29*)
FRUIT: FAITH
Second Decade: The Ascension of Our Lord (*Lk 24:50-53*)
FRUIT: HOPE
Third Decade: The Descent of the Holy Spirit at Pentecost (Acts 2:1-41)
FRUIT: LOVE OF GOD
Fourth Decade: The Assumption of Mary into Heaven
FRUIT: GRACE OF A HAPPY DEATH
Fifth Decade: The Coronation of Mary as Queen of Heaven and Earth
FRUIT: TRUST IN THE INTERCESSION OF MARY

Child Consecration

Day 1

COME, HOLY SPIRIT…

(see page 11 for prayer to the Holy Spirit)

A Garden

There once was a young girl named Daisy. She wanted very much to grow a garden. Her father loved flowers and fresh vegetables grown in the garden, and Daisy wanted to try to grow them. Her mother was a very accomplished gardener and had grown things from when she, too, was very young. Her mother had developed problems with her hands, and so they were not very strong, and she could no longer do the gardening herself. If the family was going to have fresh vegetables, then Daisy was going to have to get busy.

She had heard many things about gardening. One must start with a seed. Each seed became a different vegetable or flower. Father was the one to provide the seeds. He chose what would be grown. Seeing Daisy's excitement to help, Father gave her several small bundles of seeds. On each bundle read a different name.

Daisy had heard that soil would be needed. It was important that the soil was pure and free from

Child Consecration

disease or things that could damage the seeds. A tray was gathered with seven little clay pots. As Daisy lived in a place where the winters are cold and the growing season is relatively short, seeds often were started inside. When the plants were stronger, they were moved outside when the weather was more hospitable.

Planting began. Mother was right by little Daisy's side as Daisy placed the first seed into the soil. "Not too deep," Mother told her.

There seemed to be a perfect depth to placing the seed. Mother said that if it is too shallow, the seed might be washed away or become exposed when it is watered. When the seed was exposed and not within the soil, it was not protected and could become dried out and die. If the seed was too deep, then it might never sprout.

Once the seeds were planted, it was time to water. "Not too cold with the water," Mother told Daisy. "Warm water is best. It will help to allow the seeds to germinate. The warm water tells the seeds it is springtime."

The seed trays were placed on the radiators in the home. It was still February, and outside there was snow and wind. The radiators were busy keeping the house warm but also provided just the right amount of heat to help tell those seeds it is time to wake up and start growing. Sure enough, just as Mother had predicted, the seeds were up in less than two weeks. Little green sprouts were poking through the soil. It was very exciting!

Daisy reflected: *Mother was with me through the whole process. She had tried many things when she was learning to garden. She told me that she had tried growing the seeds only with sterile soil and adding water. She found that after a few weeks, they stopped growing. They were hungry for nutrients, but the soil didn't have any. She told me that for a long time she grew the seeds only by the window but found the plants were long and spindly and would fall over. They were trying to catch a glimpse of the light and never could get enough to make them strong. The seeds, she told me, needed lots of light—many hours, in fact—and the light made their stems strong so they would not fall over. This was important because when they were big plants and ready to make fruit or vegetables, if the stem was weak, they would fall over, and then fruit would be damaged, or the plant could die.*

There was indeed a lot to know when growing plants—too much for poor Daisy to know herself. There were many pitfalls she might fall into. But it seemed Mother had seen many things before when she was gardening herself and now always seemed to know how to avoid disaster. A long time ago, she had been as Daisy was now. Mother had learned from her parents many lessons in the garden. Father had also taught Mother many things. He had put her in charge of helping the children with their seeds. It was a good thing because it would have been much more difficult without her help.

One of the things the small house had was an attached greenhouse. It was a sort of nursery for the young seedlings. The greenhouse was heated just enough so the plants would not freeze, but not too much as heating in the winter is costly. During the day, the winter sun would come across the house and warm the little greenhouse. The top half of the walls of the greenhouse were glass, and the roof of the greenhouse was glass as well. Red Geraniums Mother had kept from last summer hung in hanging baskets. If these plants were left outside through the winter, they would have died, but in the greenhouse they were protected and flourished. In the second week of February, Mother and Daisy noticed that for a half hour at 11:00 a.m., the greenhouse became very warm and toasty from the sun. With each passing week, the time lasted longer. The days, too, were getting longer, and the seeds could sense spring was coming. The plants that had been transitioned from the radiator to the greenhouse were now growing stronger. Mother showed how the seedlings needed nutrients in order to grow, so fertilizer was given periodically.

Daisy thought back on her experiences: *It was a joy to come into the greenhouse with Mother. We looked over all our little plants. We had to be very careful not to miss watering any of the little cups. If any were forgotten, they could dry out. Small plants can't withstand being dry for very long.* Mother explained that larger plants have more of an ability to withstand such a drought, but little ones cannot. *We had so much fun in the greenhouse! We could see the snow and ice outside, but inside the greenhouse we had spring two months early. It was work to go each day to water. Yes, indeed it was hard. One*

could never overlook a seedling, or else the plant would suffer and might die. But Mother was good at helping me remember.

As the days got warmer and the snow melted, Mother told me it was time to move the plants outside. It was also becoming a little hot inside the greenhouse as the sun was getting stronger. The plants were still tender. The transition would be slow. They would be brought outside for several hours a day, then brought inside. One could do the change all at once, but Mother was gentle to the seedlings and was teaching me the same gentleness. She did not want to shock the little plants as the temperatures were still cold at night—not enough to freeze the plants, but still cold. A slow transition would allow the plants to get used to the cold temperatures and strengthen. This was something Mother called "hardening off." Once the plants were used to these temperatures, it would be time for them to go in the garden. Well, not exactly. Work had to be done to the garden to ready it for the plants. This was something that was happening all year long, so the work was not too much in the spring. Mother had been putting little vegetable scraps from the kitchen into the garden and also ash from the fireplace. This enriched the soil and provided the food the plants would need to grow. The soil needed to be loosened, and then the little plants were set into the ground.

Spring was here, and summer came upon us very quickly. It was amazing how fast time went by! The fall harvest was approaching. Father would be coming to the garden to see the progress. He would be looking for the vegetables that were his favorites. We had been watching the plants grow. Little critters came and tried to take the *vegetables, but mother had put a net over the plants so the animals could not take the fruit. We could see how the sun helped the plants grow and the rain refreshed the plants.*

Daisy was in charge of watering as the bucket was too heavy for Mother. When it did not rain, Daisy watered. It was hard work, and she was happy to see the rain clouds come and to have a day or two to rest from her work. The rain always seemed to water the plants more deeply than the watering can. Mother was very happy with little Daisy's progress. Sometimes Mother had to correct Daisy when she was not keeping up with the work. Mother would have liked to do the work herself, but she needed Daisy's hands as her own were too weak.

But fall was quickly upon them. Harvesting had begun. Each item had to be harvested in a certain way so as not to damage the plants and to allow more fruit to grow. Mother showed Daisy how to get the biggest harvest that could be attained from the seeds entrusted to Daisy by Father.

Indeed, the day arrived when Father came to the garden. He saw all in order, and on the outdoor table everything was arranged. Daisy had carried the vegetables and flowers to the table, but Mother had

Child Consecration

arranged them on the table in just a way that they might be most pleasing to Father, as she knew him so well.

Father came to the table and smiled. He was very pleased. There would be a big surprise for little Daisy for all her hard work. Father would prepare a feast from all she had grown, and Daisy would be sitting right next to Father to enjoy it.

Day 2

COME, HOLY SPIRIT...

We have a Heavenly Father who loves us. We are on a journey to reach our home, which is in Heaven. The time we spend on earth is a time of preparation to be ready to meet Our Heavenly Father face to face in Heaven after our time on earth is over. There are many roads to take throughout our life. Some are straight, while others are winding and steep. One could become lost on the journey. The Father with His heart overflowing with love for His children gave to them a Heavenly Mother. It is to her that He entrusted His children. Our Blessed Mother loves us with tenderness and compassion. She is pure as a lily and full of wisdom. Through the grace of God the Father, she can help children to find the straightest and smoothest path to our permanent home in Heaven. It is possible to reach Our Heavenly Father alone, but it is much more difficult and would take much longer.

In the story, "A Garden," Daisy, in many ways, is like each of us. Her mother represents Our Blessed Mother who is a mother to each of us individually. Daisy is little as we are little. The goal is not to try to figure out all the things we do not know. Instead, it is to turn to Our Blessed Mother and give ourselves and all we have to her. She, in turn, presents this to God in the most pleasing way as she is without blemish and full of grace. Once we put ourselves and all we have under her protection, she will guide us on our journey. We also have to place our trust in her that she always will do the best for us and that her plans are united with the will of the Father in Heaven.

Child Consecration

Indeed, to find such protection, we have to ask for it. It is through this Consecration journey that we may more fully embrace this gift that is available to us. It is a gift of protection and love from Our Mother who wants nothing more than to see all her children safe in their permanent home in Heaven.

Goal: We are loved by God, and He gave us Our Blessed Mother to help us reach our true home in Heaven.

OUR FATHER . . .

HAIL MARY . . .

GLORY BE . . .

AVE MARIS STELLA . . .

Day 3

COME, HOLY SPIRIT...

St. Louis de Montfort stated in his book *True Devotion to Mary* that "no one can find Mary who does not seek her; and no one can seek her who does not know her."[4] Our Blessed Mother Mary conceived Jesus through the Holy Spirit, one of the Three Persons of the Holy Trinity. In this way, Mary's Spouse is the Holy Spirit, Who is divine. She herself is not divine. Yet she is the only fully mortal person who was conceived without sin. Her soul is therefore a most fertile soul. Not only was she pure and without sin at her conception; she remained pure throughout her life. Through the Holy Spirit, she conceived and then bore a Son, Jesus, Who is the Second Person of the Trinity. The First Person of the Trinity is God the Father. So, there is a very special relationship between Mary and God in His Three Persons.

It is within her virginal womb that she carried Jesus. Her womb, in many ways, is like a mold, a mold of holiness. Those who have worked with clay will know how to make a perfect form. One can take away bits and pieces and try to push and pull parts of the clay to reach the desired final shape. Or one can use the more reliable way and also the quickest way to reach the form that is desired, and that is to use a mold. When the clay is placed in the mold, it is surrounded by the final shape that is sought, and when the mold is removed, the perfect shape remains. In a similar manner, Our Lady can help to mold us in holiness in a gentle and quick way, but we must ask her to help us.

Child Consecration

Goal: Our Blessed Mother Mary in her purity can help to mold us in holiness.

OUR FATHER...

HAIL MARY...

GLORY BE...

AVE MARIS STELLA...

Day 4

COME, HOLY SPIRIT...

The task that Mary was given was a great one. She raised Jesus, and as a perfect child, He was obedient to His Mother. God the Father put great confidence in Mary with His own Son. It therefore pleases God that we, likewise, place our confidence in her and submit to her. In the story "A Garden," Daisy listens to the guidance of her mother. Daisy is directed exactly how to plant the seeds that were given to her. She is reminded to water the seeds and to be about her duties. This is all done with tenderness and love. Yet there is a firmness as well. Our Blessed Mother Mary knows how precious we are to Our Lord, and she wants us always to be close to God and on the path to Heaven. Being obedient to the guidance of Our Heavenly Mother helps keep us on the straightest path to our eternal home.

Likewise, Mary puts complete trust in God. In the Bible, one of the few times Mary speaks is during the wedding feast at Cana when the bride and groom run out of wine. She asks her Son to help. He explains that His time has not yet come. Her response was to tell the servers, "Do whatever He tells you" *(Jn 2:5)*. Mary's confidence is not disappointed. Indeed, Jesus changes the water in several large stone jars into wine. The water is not turned into the common wine that had been served at the wedding. Instead, the water is turned into a choice wine superior in flavor. Jesus does not only fulfill His Mother's request; He exceeds the expectations of His Mother. We see from this example that Mary's requests are received in a special way.

Child Consecration

Goal: Jesus was obedient to Mary, and it pleases God when we too submit ourselves to Mary.

OUR FATHER . . .

HAIL MARY . . .

GLORY BE . . .

AVE MARIS STELLA . . .

Day 5

COME, HOLY SPIRIT...

"Our Blessed Lady is the means Our Lord made use of to come to us. She is also the means which we must make use of to go to Him."[5]
— St. Louis de Montfort

Mary's first role was one of a mother. It is through Our Lady with the Divine Child in her arms that the world came to know God in the person of Jesus. It was Mary who held Jesus's hand as He learned to walk. She fed Him and loved Him, and He, in turn, loved His Mother. Thus, when we want to approach Jesus, it is a good practice to come with Our Blessed Mother. For when she presents something, however small, it is most warmly received, as the hands that present it are the pure hands that cared for Our Lord.

Likewise, in our story of "A Garden," Daisy brings the fruits that were grown to the table, but it is Mother who arranged them on the table in just a way that they might be most pleasing to Father.

Child Consecration

Goal: It is pleasing to God that we come to Him with Our Blessed Mother, and that through her pure hands, our fruits are given to Him.

OUR FATHER . . .

HAIL MARY . . .

GLORY BE . . .

AVE MARIS STELLA . . .

Day 6

COME, HOLY SPIRIT...

In the story of "A Garden," we see that Mother is not able to help Daisy with her hands. In the story we are told Mother's hands are not very strong. Mother is able to stay close and guide Daisy, but Daisy is the one who must use her hands to do the work. So it is with Our Blessed Mother. She can guide us, but we are the ones God calls to work in the vineyard. Our Blessed Mother, like us, lived on earth and toiled with the difficulties of life. From Heaven, she can guide us, but the work is to be done by those still of this earth–the laborers. We are told that "[t]he harvest is abundant but the laborers are few" *(Lk* 10:2*)*. Many are called, such as when the king sent the servants to notify those invited to the banquet, but they refused to come *(cf. Mt 22:3)*. We are told repeatedly in Scripture, "Whoever has ears ought to hear" *(Mt* 11:15, *Rev* 2:29*;* cf. *Mk* 4:9, *Lk* 8:8*)*. So often we do not hear the call to the vineyard or even the call to the banquet. Our Lady is there to help us not to miss the call.

Goal: We are called to work in the vineyard, and Our Blessed Mother can help guide us in our work.

OUR FATHER ...

HAIL MARY ...

GLORY BE ...

AVE MARIS STELLA ...

Day 7

COME, HOLY SPIRIT...

How does Our Lady help us to hear Our Lord's call? She draws souls to prayer. Just as a seed needs water and nutrients, our souls need the water and food of prayer. Plants also need the warm rays of the sun. Just so, our souls thirst for the love of God. A plant deprived of sun grows weak and with the first strong wind is blown over. Those young plants that bask in the sun grow strong. Just so, a soul that draws close to the love of Our Lord grows strong. Our Lady also teaches souls to come to prayer in humility. To be humble is not to deny the good things God has done. Mary never did this. We see this in the Canticle of Mary:

> "My soul proclaims the greatness of the Lord; my spirit rejoices in God my Savior. For He has looked upon His handmaid's lowliness; behold, from now on will all ages call me blessed." *(Lk 1:46-48)*

Following in the example of Mary, we are to acknowledge our weakness and dependence on God. When God chooses to use us as an instrument, the resulting fruits are always to glorify God, and not ourselves.

Goal: Our Lady helps us to hear Our Lord's call by leading us to prayer.

OUR FATHER . . .

HAIL MARY . . .

GLORY BE . . .

AVE MARIS STELLA . . .

Day 8

COME, HOLY SPIRIT...

Devotion to Our Blessed Mother leads to a closer relationship with the Holy Spirit. St. Louis de Montfort so beautifully expressed this: "When the Holy Ghost, her Spouse, has found Mary in a soul, He flies there."[6] The *Catechism of the Catholic Church* articulates beautifully the unique relationship between Mary and the Holy Spirit:

> The Holy Spirit *prepared* Mary by His grace. (*Catechism* 722)

> In Mary, the Holy Spirit *fulfills* the plan of the Father's loving goodness. Through the Holy Spirit, the Virgin conceives and gives birth to the Son of God. By the Holy Spirit's power and her faith, her virginity became uniquely fruitful. (*Catechism* 723)

> Finally, through Mary, the Holy Spirit begins to bring men, the objects of God's merciful love, *into communion* with Christ. And the humble are always the first to accept Him. (*Catechism* 725)

We see, therefore, that children in their innocence and humility are more easily drawn into communion with Christ through Mary and the actions of the Holy Spirit.

The *Catechism* also teaches us the following:

> By this power of the Spirit, God's children can bear much fruit. He who has grafted

us onto the true vine will make us bear "the fruit of the Spirit: . . . love, joy, peace, patience, kindness, goodness, faithfulness, gentleness, self-control." "We live by the Spirit"; the more we renounce ourselves, the more we "walk by the Spirit." (*Catechism* 736)

The Spirit *prepares* men and goes out to them with His grace, in order to draw them to Christ. (*Catechism* 737)

From the beginning to the end of time, whenever God sends His Son, He always sends His Spirit: Their mission is conjoined and inseparable. (*Catechism* 743)

In the fullness of time the Holy Spirit completes in Mary all the preparations for Christ's coming among the People of God. (*Catechism* 744)

Thus, we see how the Holy Spirit works in Mary and through Mary. When we draw closer to Mary, we likewise draw closer to the Holy Spirit.

Goal: Devotion to Our Blessed Mother leads us to a closer relationship with the Holy Spirit.

OUR FATHER . . .

HAIL MARY . . .

GLORY BE . . .

AVE MARIS STELLA . . .

Day 9

COME, HOLY SPIRIT...

Our Blessed Mother also instills in those devoted to her a spirit of gratitude. Mothers are very good at reminding their children to thank those who give them gifts. We are constantly receiving gifts from God the Father, but often we do not perceive these gifts. As we develop a closer relationship with Our Blessed Mother, she helps her children to become more sensitive and aware of the gifts that flow from the Father. And after she increases our awareness of the gifts being given to us, she fills our hearts with a spirit of gratitude.

A soul that is grateful is most pleasing to God. We do not deserve all the gifts we receive, but being thankful is a small way we can show our love for Our Heavenly Father. This spirit of gratitude also calls down from Heaven a rain of even more graces and blessings. Such are the joys of a grateful soul.

Goal: Mary helps her children to see the gifts they are receiving from God and helps us to cultivate a grateful heart that is eager to thank God.

OUR FATHER...

10 HAIL MARYS...

GLORY BE...

Day 10

COME, HOLY SPIRIT...

Our Lady helps us to make good use of time. Just as a flower has a short time to bloom and then fades, our time here on earth is short. It is particularly hard to understand this when we are young. Our whole life stands before us, and time seems our friend. Yet wasted time is something that cannot be undone. We can only go forward and resolve anew to do better. But what if from a tender age Our Lady was by your side? What if she was forming you in holiness and gently guiding you to make use of your gifts given by God for His glory? How happy a soul will be in the sunset of life to look back and see a life lived to the fullest from childhood! Such is a great grace to those who have devotion to Mary from youth.

Goal: Our Lady helps us to make good use of our time.

OUR FATHER...

10 HAIL MARYS...

GLORY BE...

Day 11

COME, HOLY SPIRIT...

A gardener knows that seeds planted in pure fertile soil will yield a greater harvest than those planted in contaminated soil, which contains disease. Three times in Scripture there are references to the benefits of seeds that fall on good soil. Those seeds grown in good soil can produce crops a hundred times as great (cf. *Lk* 8:8, *Mt* 13:8, *Mk* 4:8).

In much the same way, our souls bear more fruit when they are pure than when purity is lost. Sin can be forgiven, but once a soul loses its purity, it cannot be renewed to its original glory. It can be mended, so to speak, and repaired, but it will not be the same as it was originally. If one is to think of dear Daisy and her garden, if she were able to keep the soil of her garden free from contamination and things that would harm her seeds, then she would have the opportunity to grow more fruit and vegetables to give to Father. But if the soil were to become contaminated, the seeds might still grow, but the harvest would be less. Over time the soil can be improved by heavy helpings of good things. However, it takes time and much effort. The harvest can be improved, but most often it will not reach a condition that would yield a harvest similar to that grown in pure, clean soil.

Our Blessed Mother who embodies purity watches over the innocent souls of her children with great attention. She guards purity, as she knows its great value in Heaven and the pleasure it gives the Father to see a soul pure and tending its garden. Thus when a soul Consecrates itself to Our Lady at a tender age, Our Blessed Mother has the opportunity to guard the purity of the soul more effectively.

Goal: Consecration to Our Blessed Mother at a young age helps to preserve the precious innocence and purity of one's soul.

OUR FATHER . . .

10 HAIL MARYS . . .

GLORY BE . . .

Day 12
COME, HOLY SPIRIT...

A young branch can easily be bent to the desired direction of the gardener. However, if a branch is allowed to grow unattended, it may wander in the wrong direction. If the branch remains without correction for a long time, it requires great force to move it. Likewise, if a tree has been allowed to grow in the wrong direction for considerable time, it may need to be cut to its trunk and then allowed to grow anew. This correction is much more "painful." Our soul is like a tender branch, and it is therefore of great benefit to be guided by Our Lady from a tender age. In this way, Our Lady can make the corrections gently.

Goal: While children are tender and young, they easily can be brought in the direction of holiness where they can become sturdy in faith and love.

OUR FATHER...

10 HAIL MARYS...

GLORY BE...

Day 13

COME, HOLY SPIRIT...

In the story, "A Garden," young Daisy is given seeds by her father to grow. These seeds are especially chosen for her. They are not exactly the same as the seeds given to other children. They are carefully chosen with love.

A similar story exists in the Gospels when three servants are each given talents. One servant is given five talents, one servant is given two talents, and the last servant is given one talent. We are told each was given according to his ability. Then the master went away. When he returned, he called the servants to settle accounts with them.

The servant to whom he had given five brought the original talents as well as five more. The master congratulated the servant, "Well done, my good and faithful servant. Since you were faithful in small matters, I will give you great responsibilities. Come, share your master's joy" *(Mt 25:21)*.

When the servant to whom the master had given two approached, he brought two additional talents. To him the master said, "Well done, my good and faithful servant. Since you were faithful in small matters, I will give you great responsibilities. Come, share your master's joy" *(Mt 25:23)*.

Tomorrow we will find out what became of the third servant.

Goal: Each seed or talent is given according to our ability, and we will be held accountable as to what we have done with our gifts.

OUR FATHER . . .

10 HAIL MARYS . . .

GLORY BE . . .

Day 14

COME, HOLY SPIRIT...

The last servant who had received the one talent approached the master. Addressing the master, he said, "I knew you were a demanding person, harvesting where you did not plant and gathering where you did not scatter; so out of fear I went off and buried your talent in the ground. Here it is back" *(Mt 25:24-25)*.

His master responded, "You wicked, lazy servant! So you knew that I harvest where I did not plant and gather where I did not scatter? Should you not then have put my money in the bank so that I could have got it back with interest on my return? Now then! Take the talent from him and give it to the one with ten. For to everyone who has, more will be given and he will grow rich; but from the one who has not, even what he has will be taken away. And throw this useless servant into the darkness outside, where there will be wailing and grinding of teeth" *(Mt 25:26-30)*.

Goal: The Father expects to harvest where He did not sow.

OUR FATHER...

10 HAIL MARYS...

GLORY BE...

Day 15

COME, HOLY SPIRIT...

How can one help the Father to harvest where He did not sow? The answer lies in the seed. Let us think of our dear Daisy from our story, "A Garden." Her father gave her several bags of seeds. When those are planted, they can yield a harvest. For example, when lettuce is planted, one can harvest the leaves of the lettuce to eat in a salad. If, however, you leave the lettuce plant, it will send up a tall stalk, will flower, and will make seeds of its own. Many people pull up the lettuce plant before it makes seeds because the leaves of the lettuce plant become bitter once it sends up a stalk and flowers. If the plant is removed, there is only one harvest. If, however, the plant remains and is allowed to produce its own seeds, each seed can yield a new plant. Every seed of the lettuce plant forms what looks like short white hairs. These act as sails.

When the wind blows, the seeds take flight, and the destination is determined by the direction of the wind. The result is that the seed may fall in another person's yard. It may grow and produce a harvest of its own, such as more lettuce. If the plant is left for the whole season, it can again make its own seeds, and these can be taken by the wind yet farther.

In much the same way, a soul can reap harvests for many years even after it is no longer on earth. One can think of parents. They sow the seeds of love and faith in the hearts of their children. The parents also may use the gifts God has given them to show kindness and love to their neighbor. The effects of this may bring others to do acts of love and kindness and to witness faith in the way they observed it in the original parents. Thus when the original parents are gone, a harvest for the Lord may persist from the original seeds that were given to the parents.

Jesus states, "It was not you who chose Me, but I who chose you and appointed you to go and bear fruit that will remain, so that whatever you ask the Father in My Name He may give you. This I command you: love one another" *(Jn* 15:16-17*).* Thus one can see that the expectation God has is not unreasonable. If we nourish the seeds God gives us with prayer and we do not hide our light under a bushel *(cf. Mt* 5:15*),* then in a beautiful way we may play a part in a harvest that will remain.

Goal: The seeds God gives us can yield harvests for many years and have far-reaching effects beyond each of us.

OUR FATHER . . .

10 HAIL MARYS . . .

GLORY BE . . .

Day 16

COME, HOLY SPIRIT...

The fruits that we grow we do not want to lose while we harvest others. This can happen if the fruits are not stored in safety. In the story, "A Garden," we are told that "[l]ittle critters came and tried to take the vegetables." Something similar can happen to us. During our time here on earth, through our prayers, love, and sacrifices, we can accumulate fruits that we wish to give to the Father. When we store our fruits on earth, they can decay and, worse yet, be taken.

Yet just as the mother in our story, "A Garden," protected the vegetables from being taken by placing a net over them, so, too, Our Blessed Mother can protect all we have gathered to give to God. How wise is the child that from a young age gives all that he or she harvests to Our Blessed Mother for safe keeping. What joy there will be when the Father comes at harvest time and all is ready and safe!

Child Consecration

Goal: Let us give all our fruits and treasures to Mary that she may keep them safe.

CREED...

OUR FATHER...

10 HAIL MARYS...

GLORY BE...

Day 17

COME, HOLY SPIRIT...

Not only do we want our treasures to be safe from thieves; our souls are also at risk of being lost due to sin. Our Lady has often been likened to an ark. In the *Catechism of the Catholic Church*, it states:

> Mary is full of grace because the Lord is with her.... Mary, in whom the Lord Himself has just made His dwelling, is the daughter of Zion in person, the Ark of the Covenant, the place where the glory of the Lord dwells. She is "the dwelling of God ... with men." Full of grace, Mary is wholly given over to Him Who has come to dwell in her and Whom she is about to give to the world.
> (*Catechism* 2676)

Indeed, Mary is the Ark of the Covenant—carrying Jesus in her virginal womb. Likewise, she can be an ark to each of us as well. She is a Noah's Ark: a place of refuge for our souls. We have only to run to her and put ourselves under her protection. She gladly opens the door to each of us. But we must go to her and ask for such protection as a little child goes to his mother and asks for help.

Goal: Mary is like Noah's Ark for our souls.

CREED...

OUR FATHER...

10 HAIL MARYS...

GLORY BE...

Day 18

COME, HOLY SPIRIT...

When Mary has struck her roots in a soul, she produces the marvels of grace.[7]
— St. Louis de Montfort

It is important for a young plant to send down deep roots. Winds and harsh weather may beat against the tender plant, and if the roots are shallow, they will be uprooted and die. Yet if the roots are watered deeply on a regular basis, they will go very deep. In a similar way, when the roots of virtue and faith are watered by prayer and grace each day, the roots go deeper in a soul. Later when suffering and temptation come, the plant is deeply rooted and weathers the storms. When a soul Consecrates itself to Our Blessed Mother, it invites Our Lady to establish her roots in the soul and to encourage the roots of faith and virtue to deepen and flourish.

Goal: We wish to have Mary set deep roots in our souls.

CREED...

OUR FATHER...

10 HAIL MARYS...

GLORY BE...

Day 19

COME, HOLY SPIRIT...

We do not want to stand before God at the end of our life and have Him show us all that we could have achieved. How sad it would be to see the multitude of fruits and vegetables we could have harvested, and yet we stand with just a few or worse yet . . . nothing. There will be no time to go back and retrace our steps and do things differently. But what if we had such a wise and perfect perspective when we set out on our journey . . . before any time was lost? What if we had the wisdom of a person who had lived their whole life when yet we were tiny and just starting out? To have Our Blessed Mother lead us is to have a guide who has not only the perspective of a life already lived, but also the perspective from Heaven where things are seen through the lens of truth.

Our Blessed Mother who is in Heaven also has the ability to see those dangers where we might fall and be spiritually hurt. While we walk through a thick forest where pitfalls lie before us, she has full view of these dangers and can gently guide us around them in safety. How wonderful to have someone with a perfect view watching out for us and leading us to the goal we seek which is union with God and eternity in Heaven!

Child Consecration

Goal: Our Blessed Mother can see potential dangers that lie before each of us—how wise is the soul that asks Our Lady to guide it through life!

CREED...

OUR FATHER...

10 HAIL MARYS...

GLORY BE...

Day 20

COME, HOLY SPIRIT...

Gentleness. In the story, "A Garden," Mother teaches Daisy a gentleness in growing the seedlings. When they are tender and young sprouts, they are kept free from every danger on the warm radiator of the house. As the sun is on them by the window, they strengthen. They are protected so that nothing from outside the little house is able to reach them. As the seedlings grow, they are ready for more sun and are brought to the greenhouse. There the stems thicken, and the tiny plants grow stronger. Still, they are protected from the dangers outside the greenhouse.

Then in the process gardeners call "hardening off," the seedlings are brought out for short times outside. Slowly the young plants are introduced to the world. This means there is an opportunity for critters to have access to the plants and also for cold and strong winds and rain to bear down upon the plants. Once the hardening off process is complete, the seedlings are planted in the garden outside where they can grow much bigger and begin to set fruit. That fruit, which they produce, can in turn create seeds that have the potential to multiply the harvest for seasons to come.

Mother shows us how slowly a young plant is introduced to the world. When a plant is under her care, she does everything purposefully and gently and always for the best of the plant. In the same way, Our Blessed Mother treats her children. She keeps them in her nursery while they are small. Over time as their faith strengthens, she exposes them to experiences outside the nursery until they are strong enough to stand firm in virtue within the world. Despite the wind of temptation, her children are not uprooted because they have slowly grown sturdy in faith under her care.

Goal: Our Lady will guard her tender souls with gentleness and care as they are strengthened in virtue and faith.

CREED...

OUR FATHER...

10 HAIL MARYS...

GLORY BE...

Day 21

COME, HOLY SPIRIT...

What are our treasures? We have spoken about the value of protecting our fruits and treasures, but what exactly are these? What are we accumulating? If our focus is on the world and worldly things, we may be accumulating things that are only of this world and that can decay. These things have no eternal value. Yet here again, Our Lady helps to guide us to see the true treasures. The things that will remain are love and acts of love. It is love that will open to us the Kingdom of Heaven. Our Lady reminds us to seek the pleasure of the Father, not our own pleasures. What is the pleasure or wish of the Father? It is that we love God with all our heart and with all our soul and with all our mind and with all our strength, and that we love our neighbor as ourself. There is no greater commandment than these (cf. *Mk* 12:30-31).

If we seek as our goal to please God and follow His Will, then we will have fruits and treasures that have meaning to God. If we are obedient to Him and work hard, then our fruits will multiply.

As Our Lord taught, "Do not store up for yourselves treasures on earth, where moth and decay destroy, and thieves break in and steal. But store up treasures in Heaven, where neither moth nor decay destroys, nor thieves break in and steal. For where your treasure is, there also will your heart be" (*Mt* 6:19-21).

Goal: Our Lady shows us the treasures that have eternal value.

CREED . . .

OUR FATHER . . .

10 HAIL MARYS. . .

GLORY BE . . .

Day 22

COME, HOLY SPIRIT...

One thing we know about seeds is that they need to die in order to bear fruit. Our Lord tells us, "Amen, amen, I say to you, unless a grain of wheat falls to the ground and dies, it remains just a grain of wheat; but if it dies, it produces much fruit" *(Jn 12:24)*. St. Louis de Montfort states that "we need Mary in order to die to ourselves."[8] By our own nature we are weak, inconstant, and prone toward vanity and pride. Our hearts are hard. Yet Our Blessed Mother is constant, unwavering, humble, pure, and full of love. Through Our Lady and her Spouse, the Holy Spirit, we can see, to the extent it is possible, our lowliness and dependence on God. For when we see our lowliness and look to Our Lord to supply all we are lacking, this unlocks a torrent of grace that helps to sanctify us.

Indeed, with the help of Our Lady, if we can turn our focus from ourselves and direct all our focus to God, then God can bring fruit through us. St. Thérèse, the Little Flower, through her "little way" provides a beautiful example of dying to oneself each day. She would find little sacrifices throughout the day to give to Our Lord. If there was a person Thérèse would prefer to avoid, she instead offered a big smile to this person or helped them. She began with little things like folding the mantles that the sisters left behind and providing little services to them. The Little Flower took all these as opportunities to choose love even when it was contrary to her natural inclination. In this way, she continued to reject her will and, instead, embraced the will of God, thus dying to herself.

Goal: We need Mary to help us die to ourselves.

CREED . . .

OUR FATHER . . .

10 HAIL MARYS. . .

GLORY BE . . .

Day 23

COME, HOLY SPIRIT...

Some have observed that those who have a strong devotion to Mary still experience great suffering on earth. It has even been stated that those with a strong devotion seem to suffer more than those with a lesser devotion to the Mother of God. St. Louis de Montfort responded to this observation: "It is quite true that the most faithful servants of the Blessed Virgin, being also her greatest favorites, receive from her the greatest graces and favors of Heaven, which are crosses." However, St. Louis de Montfort maintains that "it is also the servants of Mary who carry these crosses with more ease, more merit and more glory. That which would stay the progress of another a thousand times over, or perhaps would make him fall, does not once stop their steps, but rather enables them to advance."[9] Our Lady makes these crosses gladly acceptable and more sweet.

It is helpful to share an example from the garden. The pink gooseberry bush has small pink fruit that are delicious. However, no birds or other animals try to eat them because of sharp thorns that extend from the branches near the fruit. If a person were to pick the fruit, he or she would invariably prick their fingers. In the spiritual sense, when a soul Consecrates itself to Our Lady, this makes the harvesting of such fruit possible and even joyful. Our Lady helps one not to notice the prick of the fingers that comes from taking the fruit. Instead, the soul is so absorbed in the act of working in the vineyard of the Lord and harvesting that the pricks of the finger go almost unnoticed. Yes, there is pain, but the joy of gathering the harvest for Our Lord makes these efforts sweet. Indeed, those who may not have such a devotion to Our Lady may never be sent to harvest among thorns, but those who do have such a devotion and are able to do such work await great glory in Heaven for doing that which was, by earthly standards, more difficult.

Goal: Our Lady prepares the crosses of those devoted to her in such a way as to make them wholly acceptable and even sweet.

CREED . . .

OUR FATHER . . .

10 HAIL MARYS . . .

GLORY BE . . .

Day 24

COME, HOLY SPIRIT...

Sanctity is something children in particular can attain as it is most easily reached through simplicity. Once when St. Thérèse was participating in recreation, a saintly Novice Mistress spoke to her. She stated, "My child, it seems to me you don't have very much to tell your Superiors." Thérèse asked why the Mother thought this. The nun responded, "Because your soul is extremely *simple*, but when you will be perfect, you will be even *more simple*; the closer one approaches to God, the simpler one becomes." St. Thérèse relates, "The good Mother was right."[10]

Scripture also confirms the importance of remaining simple. In the Gospel of Matthew, Jesus states, "I give praise to You, Father, Lord of Heaven and earth, for although You have hidden these things from the wise and the learned You have revealed them to the childlike" *(Mt 11:25)*. In the Gospel of Mark, Our Lord rebukes the Apostles for trying to keep the children from Him. He states, "Let the children come to me, do not prevent them, for the Kingdom of God belongs to such as these. Amen, I say to you, whoever does not accept the Kingdom of God like a child will not enter it" *(Mk 10:14-15)*.

Goal: Our Lord calls children in particular to come to Him and desires simplicity in a soul.

CREED . . .

OUR FATHER . . .

10 HAIL MARYS . . .

GLORY BE . . .

Day 25

COME, HOLY SPIRIT...

Up until today we have spoken about devotion to Mary and how it leads to her Son, Jesus. Today we will focus on Jesus Who is the ultimate end we seek in this Consecration journey. It is interesting that we use the word "seek" as it is Jesus Who seeks us. From the time we were fashioned in our mother's womb, He knew us (cf. *Jer* 1:5). He not only waits for us, but also pursues us with His love. What is He looking for, one might ask? He is looking for our love. We are created out of love for the purpose of loving. Yet we are given free will to love or to turn away from that love that is offered to us. If Jesus does not have our love, no one can replace it–for the love each of us offers is unique. In the Gospel of John, Jesus identifies Himself as the Good Shepherd *(cf. Jn* 10:11) Who would leave ninety-nine sheep to find the one lost sheep. He values us so much that He would leave ninety-nine to find the lost one *(cf. Mt* 18:12-14*)*.

Just as a field of wildflowers would not hold the same beauty if every flower were the same, just so each flower, whether violet or even the simple daisy, is precious and contributes to the glory of God. It is the same with our love. It is said, in the Gospel of Matthew, that Our Lord had "nowhere to rest His head" *(Mt* 8:20*)*. When we love Jesus, our heart becomes a place of rest where He can put His head.

Goal: Jesus wants our love.

PRAY THE ROSARY

Day 26

COME, HOLY SPIRIT...

We should not only have confidence in Mary, but also in the One to Whom she leads us: Jesus. In the Gospel of Matthew, we are reassured by Our Lord,

"Do not worry about your life, what you will eat [or drink], or about your body, what you will wear. Is not life more than food and the body more than clothing? Look at the birds in the sky; they do not sow or reap, they gather nothing into barns, yet your Heavenly Father feeds them. Are not you more important than they? Can any of you by worrying add a single moment to your life-span? Why are you anxious about clothes? Learn from the way the wild flowers grow. They do not work or spin. But I tell you that not even Solomon in all his splendor was clothed like one of them. If God so clothes the grass of the field, which grows today and is thrown into the oven tomorrow, will he not much more provide for you, O you of little faith? So do not worry and say, 'What are we to eat?' or 'What are we to drink?' or 'What are we to wear?' All these things the pagans seek. Your Heavenly Father knows that you need them all. But seek first the Kingdom [of God] and his righteousness, and all these things will be given you besides. Do not worry about tomorrow; tomorrow will take care of itself. Sufficient for a day is its own evil." *(Mt 6:25-34)*

Thomas à Kempis states, "The beginning of temptation lies in a wavering mind and little trust in God."[11] When we worry, we begin to exhibit pride since worrying is rooted in the idea that we are in control. When we acknowledge that we are not in control, the soul can surrender and become docile to the Will of God. If we have confidence and trust in God, we are secure and have nothing to fear.

Goal: We must place our complete trust in God and not worry.

PRAY THE ROSARY

Day 27

COME, HOLY SPIRIT...

"Ask and it will be given to you; seek and you will find; knock and the door will be opened to you. For everyone who asks, receives; and the one who seeks, finds; and to the one who knocks, the door will be opened."
— Matthew 7:7-8

Jesus desires that we come to Him and share our problems. Jesus explains His willingness to answer our prayers: "Which one of you would hand his son a stone when he asks for a loaf of bread, or a snake when he asks for a fish? If you then, who are wicked, know how to give good gifts to your children, how much more will your Heavenly Father give good things to those who ask Him" *(Mt 7:9-11)*.

We are also told to persist with our prayers. Jesus explains, "Suppose one of you has a friend to whom he goes at midnight and says, 'Friend, lend me three loaves of bread, for a friend of mine has arrived at my house from a journey and I have nothing to offer him,' and he says in reply from within, 'Do not bother me; the door has already been locked and my children and I are already in bed. I cannot get up to give you anything'" *(Lk 11:5-7)*. But Jesus then goes on to explain that though the man "does not get up to give him the loaves because of their friendship, he will get up to give him whatever he needs because of his persistence" *(Lk 11:8)*.

Goal: Have recourse to prayer, and persist in your prayers.

PRAY THE ROSARY

Day 28

COME, HOLY SPIRIT...

O, God Whose Providence never fails in its design.[12]
— *Roman Missal*

Indeed, God is watching each detail of our life. Difficulties and hardships are permitted by God, but this does not mean He has abandoned us or does not love us. On the contrary, suffering is a gift given to souls who are especially dear to Him. Suffering is a way Our Lord uses to draw us closer to Himself. It is a way of purifying our love for Him. We should not worry and question the ways of God, "[f]or the wisdom of this world is foolishness in the eyes of God" *(1Cor* 3:19). Suffering is also a way we can participate with God in the redemption of other souls, which is a precious gift. Thus we should have confidence in the Providence of God. A true story from my own garden illustrates this point.

Several years ago we began to see a tomato plant growing in the crack between where the front cement walk meets brick stairs to the front door. It appeared that a seed had fallen in the crack the previous summer, possibly from one of the plants that had been growing in our front planters. Not much water could get in the crack, but as the plant grew under the canopy of a mature tree, it did not dry out like the plants in the full sun. The squirrels that usually patrol the garden did not see the tomato plant growing in this unusual place. Thus what seemed like an unfortunate situation—a seed falling in a small crack in the front walk—turned out to yield a surprisingly good harvest. Such is our life. Things may come that we do not understand, such as difficulty and trial. Even though the seed had a much less hospitable home in the crack than did the plants in the large garden, the little plant persisted and yielded more than those growing in the garden. We should put our trust in God because He knows what is best for us, and all is there for our sanctification.

Goal: Trust in the Providence of God, and accept difficulties and sufferings.

PRAY THE ROSARY

Day 29

COME, HOLY SPIRIT...

Jesus tells us, "I am the true vine" *(Jn* 15:1*)*. He goes on to ask,

> "Remain in me, as I remain in you. Just as a branch cannot bear fruit on its own unless it remains on the vine, so neither can you unless you remain in me. I am the vine, you are the branches. Whoever remains in me and I in him will bear much fruit, because without me you can do nothing. Anyone who does not remain in me will be thrown out like a branch and wither; people will gather them and throw them into a fire and they will be burned. If you remain in me and my words remain in you, ask for whatever you want and it will be done for you." *(Jn* 15: 4-7*)*

We can remain in Jesus when we follow God's commandments. We also must recognize that we are dependent on God and that by ourselves we are nothing. It pleases God for us to bring all our concerns to Him. We draw our strength from Him just as a branch receives nourishment from the vine.

Goal: We cannot bear fruit alone; we need to remain in God to bear fruit.

PRAY THE ROSARY

Day 30

COME, HOLY SPIRIT...

"Come to me, all you who labor and are burdened, and I will give you rest. Take my yoke upon you and learn from me, for I am meek and humble of heart; and you will find rest for your selves. For my yoke is easy, and my burden light."
— Matthew 11:28-30

Jesus is the Good Shepherd. He cares for us. He lifts us up when we have fallen. He leads us beside restful waters and refreshes our souls. Even in the darkest valley, we have nothing to fear. With His rod and His staff, He comforts us. He prepares a table before us in the presence of our enemies. He anoints our head with oil. Our cup overflows. Goodness and love will follow us all the days of our lives (cf. *Psalm* 23).

Goal: Let us come and rest with Our Lord.

PRAY THE ROSARY

Day 31

COME, HOLY SPIRIT...

> If, then, we establish solid devotion to our Blessed Lady, it is only to establish more perfectly devotion to Jesus Christ, and to provide an easy and secure means for finding Jesus Christ. [13]
>
> — St. Louis de Montfort

Our Lady in her humility wants none of the attention for herself. Although she has been crowned Queen of Heaven and Earth, she has lost nothing of her simplicity. She has remained small. She has followed the words of St. John the Baptist: "He must increase; I must decrease" *(Jn 3:30)*. As we saw with little Daisy, Mother did not want Father to lavish attention on her when the harvest was presented. We do not hear about Mother after Father arrives. It is for little Daisy to receive praise from her father and participate in the feast that is prepared from her harvest.

So there is no worry that giving all we have to Mary will somehow take away from any of the glory we wish to pay to God or receive when we stand before the Heavenly Father. For as God has said, "I will honor those who honor Me" *(1 Sam 2:30)*. It indeed glorifies God when we prepare ourselves and our harvest under the direction of Our Blessed Mother. It was Mary who states, "My soul proclaims the greatness of the Lord; my spirit rejoices in God my Savior" *(Lk 1:46-47)*.

On the cover of this book, we see Mary presenting the Child Jesus to us. Within the Gospels, Our Lord reassures us with His recurring words: "Do not be afraid" *(Jn 6:20; cf. Mt 10:26, Jn 14:27).* Indeed, God wants us never to be scared to approach Him. Through the Lord's mother, we meet Jesus first as a child in her arms. We are called to draw near. Our Lord first came to us on earth, small as a child. He came in a stable through humble beginnings. Simple shepherds came to pay Him homage even before kings knelt to do the same. All this, it seems, is to allow us to feel, as small children, that we are invited to draw near. Through Mary we are brought to the crib of Jesus where we can honor Him.

Goal: Devotion to Our Lady leads to glorifying Jesus.

PRAY THE ROSARY

Day 32

COME, HOLY SPIRIT...

"Holy Father, keep them in your name that you have given me, so that they may be one just as we are one."

— John 17:11

The *Catechism* teaches us, "*The Trinity is One*. We do not confess three Gods, but one God in Three Persons" *(Catechism 253)*. We further know "God is love: Father, Son and Holy Spirit. God freely wills to communicate the glory of His blessed life. Such is the 'plan of His loving kindness'" *(Catechism 257)*. As we discussed yesterday, Our Lady leads us to her Son, but since Jesus is one with the Father and the Holy Spirit, this Consecration journey leads us to be one with God in His Three Persons.

Goal: The Consecration journey ends with Jesus, and through Jesus we wish to be one with the Father, Son, and Holy Spirit.

PRAY THE ROSARY

Child Consecration

Day 33

COME, HOLY SPIRIT...

Fall was quickly upon them. Harvesting had begun. Each item had to be harvested in a certain way so as not to damage the plants and to allow more fruit to grow. Mother showed Daisy how to get the biggest harvest that could be attained from the seeds entrusted to Daisy by Father.

Indeed, the day arrived when Father came to the garden. He saw all in order, and on the outdoor table everything was arranged. Daisy had carried the vegetables and flowers to the table, but Mother had arranged them on the table in just a way that they might be most pleasing to Father, as she knew him so well.

Father came to the table and smiled. He was very pleased. There would be a big surprise for little Daisy for all her hard work. Father would prepare a feast from all she had grown, and Daisy would be sitting right next to Father to enjoy it.

PRAY THE ROSARY

Recommendations for Consecration Day

If possible, attend Mass on the day of your Consecration, and make your Consecration following Mass. Confession is also recommended prior to Consecration, if possible. As a special tribute to Jesus Christ and Our Blessed Mother, consider offering a special gift to Them. This could be a wildflower that is placed at the foot of the Cross. It could be a candle that is lit in Their honor. Or it could be almsgiving. One might consider giving up something that day as an act of sacrifice. Whatever is given, however small, should be given with love. In this way, it will have immense value to God and His mother, Mary.

Day 34
Consecration Day

COME, HOLY SPIRIT...

"I belong entirely to you, dear Mother, and all that I have is yours. . . . O Mary, I take you for my all; give me your heart."[14]

- St. Louis de Montfort

The above quotation was the inspiration for the Papal Motto of St. Pope John Paul II: "Totus tuus." For our Consecration, we will include this passage within the Consecration prayer:

Recite the following:

I, (Name), renounce satan and give myself entirely to Jesus Christ through the Immaculate Heart of Mary.

Dear Mary, I belong entirely to you, and all that I have is yours. I take you for my all. Mary, I give you my heart. O Mary, please give me your heart. I Consecrate to you, Mother Mary, my body and soul as well as my good deeds, both interior and exterior; and the value of my good actions past, present, and future. May my hands be the extended hands of Jesus and of you, Mary. May all be for the Glory of God. Amen.

Child Consecration

Then say this abbreviated version of the Consecration. It is an entrustment to Mary who leads us to Jesus. The entrustment is repeated slowly three times and should ideally be read aloud:

I belong entirely to you, dear Mother, and all that I have is yours. O Mary, I take you for my all; give me your heart. Amen.

PRAY THE ROSARY

Beyond Consecration

Praise Jesus! You have completed your Consecration. It is recommended to renew this Consecration each year at the same time by repeating the 33 days of preparation followed by renewal of one's Consecration.

In addition, consider saying the abbreviated version of the Consecration daily:

> *I belong entirely to you, dear Mother, and all that I have is yours. O Mary, I take you for my all; give me your heart. Amen.*

Indeed, going forward following this journey, we want to be fruitful. We are told in the Gospel, "Every good tree bears good fruit . . . . Every tree that does not bear good fruit will be cut down" *(Mt 7:17,19).*

Through our Consecration, we have put ourselves under the care of Our Blessed Mother. We have promised to give her everything, and in turn, she offers us great protection and love. We have set out on a road of purification and sanctification so that we may pass smoothly through the narrow gate. This means daily efforts to live the Will of God in our lives. Following Mary's example, we should try to live a simple, humble life while not concerning ourselves too much with the difficulties that come. These difficulties will pass.

We must pray a great deal! St. Louis de Montfort states, "The Hail Mary is a Heavenly dew which fertilizes the soul."[15] Therefore, if we cultivate a practice of prayer, this helps us become more fruitful. The last nine days of the Consecration involved daily prayer of the Rosary.

We recommend continuation of this daily practice.

In addition to praying at home, it is also extremely helpful to participate in a prayer group such as the Children's Rosary. This is a prayer group movement for children where the children come together in parishes, schools, or orphanages to pray the Rosary as a prayer group. If there is not a group near you, consider starting one. More information can be found at the group's website:

childrensrosary.org

References

All Bible references were taken from the New American Bible Revised Edition (New Jersey: Catholic Book Publishing Corp, 1986). All *Catechism* quotations were taken from the *Catechism of the Catholic Church* (New York: Doubleday, 1994).

1. St. Louis de Montfort, *True Devotion to Mary*, trans. Fr. Frederick Faber, D.D. (Rockford, Illinois: TAN Books, 1985), 66.

2. St. Thérèse of Lisieux, *Story of a Soul: The Autobiography of St. Thérèse of Lisieux*, 3rd ed., trans. John Clarke, O.C.D. (Washington, D.C.: ICS Publications, 1996) 112, 113.

3. St. John Bosco, *Forty Dreams of St. John Bosco: The Apostle of Youth: From the Biographical Memoirs of St. John Bosco*, ed. Fr. J Bacchiarello, S.D.B. (Charlotte, North Carolina: TAN Books, 2014), 66.

4. St. Louis de Montfort, *True Devotion to Mary*, 29.

5. St. Augustine, *Sermo* 113 in *Nativit. Domini* (inter opera Sti. Augustini).

6. St. Louis de Montfort, *True Devotion to Mary*, 21.

7. St. Louis de Montfort, *True Devotion to Mary*, 21.

8. St. Louis de Montfort, *True Devotion to Mary*, 48.

9. St. Louis de Montfort, *True Devotion to Mary*, 97.

10. St. Thérèse of Lisieux, *Story of a Soul: The Autobiography of St. Thérèse of Lisieux*, 151.

11. Thomas à Kempis, *The Imitation of Christ* (Huntington, Indiana: Our Sunday Visitor Publishing Division, 2018), 14.

12. *Roman Missal* [Third Typical Edition, Ritual Edition, 2011], 469.

13. St. Louis de Montfort, *True Devotion to Mary*, 38.

14. St. Louis Marie de Montfort, *True Devotion to the Blessed Virgin*, (Montfort Missionaries, 2002), 53, accessed Sept. 15, 2020, http://www.montfort.org/content/uploads/pdf/PDF_EN_26_1.pdf.

15. St. Louis de Montfort, *True Devotion to Mary*, 159.

Acknowledgments

A special thank you to my husband and family for their support of this project. Thank you to my son Asher Kaufman who was ten years old when I began writing this book. He helped tremendously through his prayers and encouragement. Thank you to Dom Cassian Aylward, O.S.B. who provided critical review of the manuscript. I humbly thank Roger McCaffrey for his advice. Thank you to Arlene Roemer da Feltre for serving as our copy editor. You put all of your heart and talent into this project, and I thank you. I extend my gratitude to Nick DiSantis for his patience and guidance through the publishing process. Lastly, thank you to my mom who shared her faith and love of Our Blessed Mother with me.

Author

Blythe Marie Kaufman is a wife, mother of three children, dentist, and Associate Professor at the University of Connecticut School of Dental Medicine. She is the founder of the Children's Rosary, an international prayer group movement for children. She is the author of the book *Children's Rosary: A Prayer Group Movement for Children*.

Illustrator

Abigail Ryan, a member of the Children's Rosary, painted the illustrations included in this book. Abigail has a passion for painting and sharing her faith. She began with the cover illustration at age nine and painted the remaining illustrations over a span of two years, with the last being done when she was eleven years old. Abigail lives on a small farm in Wisconsin with her father, mother, and six siblings. Abigail is a big help to her mother in the family garden and also helps, along with her siblings, to care for the family's goats; chickens; and her pet bunny, Isabelle.